The Case
for
Nation Formation

Brooks Robinson

BlackEconomics.org
Brooks B. Robinson
P.O. Box 8848
Honolulu, HI 96830-8848

ISBN-13: 978-1540441164
ISBN-10: 1540441164

Dedication

To my lovely and loving wife, WCSR.

Preface

Now that Donald Trump is President of the United States (US), Black Americans are warranted in responding to the nation's unusual and unexpected political-economy by considering alternatives that will produce the most favorable future outcomes for us.

This collection of seven commentaries seeks to motivate Black Americans (the smaller nation) to undertake renewed consideration of nation formation within the context of the broader nation in this 21st century.

Given the US mentality that was reflected in the 2016 presidential election results, Black Americans should see clearly that we have nothing to lose and everything to gain by pushing forward on nation formation—however configured.

We should also recognize that our failure to be seriously concerned about our future in America, and our refusal to organize in order to leverage our power effectively can produce unintended results.

Fortunately, Black Americans may have just enough time to muster, rally to assemble a plan, and begin to implement that plan before the new era that is to be ushered in by Trump begins to unfold systematically.

Words to the wise should be sufficient. If they are not, then Black Americans may find ourselves paying a price that is too onerous to bear.

To avoid such consequences, let us collaborate to try something new and different by operationalizing the case for nation formation.

Table of Contents

1. The "Case for Reparations" leads to the "Case for Nation Formation."

   - Coates' "The Case for Reparations" attracted a great deal of attention in the US and around the world. But did it say clearly what Black Americans should receive as compensation? What comes immediately to mind is that there will be a wealth transfer under reparations, and that Black Americans should use that wealth transfer to separate from a racist America; i.e., we should form our own new nation.

Ta-Nehisi Coates' 2014 article in the *Atlantic Magazine* entitled "The Case for Reparations" is one of the most powerful economic historical articles ever written about America's injustices to Black Americans.[1] Indeed, if you have not read the article, then you are doing yourself a great injustice. The article does not break new ground, but it does elaborate very well how the American economic system, buttressed—and in certain cases aided—by the US government and its laws, permitted White American business to exploit and defraud Black Americans for self-enrichment. Yet the article does not, and was not intended to, delineate the compensation that Black Americans should receive as reparatory justice.

Unfortunately, this set of seven commentaries, too, will not place a price on Black American reparatory justice—at least in dollar terms. But we do place a price on reparatory justice

---

[1] Ta-Nehisi Coates. (2014) "The Case for Reparations." *Atlantic Magazine*. June. Retrieved from the Internet on October 3, 2016; http://www.theatlantic.com/magazine/archive/2014/06/the-case-forreparations/361631/.

for Black Americans with respect to the actions that Black Americans should take as a direct result of the reparatory justice that will be imposed one day. What the Coates article does so beautifully is elaborate the mainly economic wrongs that have been perpetrated against us, such that even a deaf, dumb, and blind person can see that America has never had our best interest at heart—only its own. Consequently, like a child with an abusive parent, we should rush to separate from the abusing parent.

Given that reality, as opposed to hankering to remain part of the US, we should be propelled to extricate ourselves from such a poisonous environment with the aspiration of identifying a safe, secure, and healthy environment in which to live as a people. The Coates article and these commentaries are not about White Americans hating Black Americans, and they most certainly are not about Black Americans hating White Americans—although we have every reason to do so. At bottom, White Americans have done, and are doing, simply what business minded people do in a capitalist-based economic, social, and political system; they squeeze out as much wealth as possible for themselves at the expense of all factors that are at their disposal in the system. They have been, and are, very heavy-handed and egregiously cruel in the way they have executed the process, and one can wonder what type of mentality is required to commit such heinous acts. At the same time, Black Americans must understand that, if White Americans had not been so cold, cruel, and evil, then there is no question that Black Americans would have escaped by this time. It took the imposition of pain and suffering upon us to generate the fear that caused us to succumb to the injustice. Given an opportunity to escape, like a hare who is about to be ensnared by a venomous reptile, we should run as fast as possible away from the clutches of the reptile when it is temporarily distracted—in this case, being brought to its senses concerning its moral debt to Black Americans. Once we have achieved a safe distance and grown to full maturity as a free people, then we can turn our attention to assisting the world in defanging the reptile.

What Black Americans must come to understand is that our very future as a people—as we are known today—depends on our exodus from the US. Just as a frog does not perceive that the temperature of the water is rising toward the boiling point, it is difficult for us to discern that the scientific and technological matrix in which we live is purposely separating the productive and conforming from the unproductive and nonconforming with a phase-out plan for the latter. As the American society charges ahead toward artificiality (technology and artificial intelligence), it only wants to retain those who can adapt well to the new system that is coming into phase. Neither all Blacks nor all Whites will be selected to take the final steps of the journey. Therefore, if we want to save as many Black Americans as possible, then we must opt out now, and seek to build our own separate nation and operationalize our own timetable for scientific and technological advancement.

Black Americans have never held full participatory, let alone veto, power in the American system. As educational and social activist Boyce Watkins comments from time-to-time, we have always been pawns on White America's chess board. Therefore, we should not be surprised when decisions are made and actions are taken that are not in our best interest. Understanding this, we should begin to plan now to use any potential future wealth transfer that comes in the form of reparations as a springboard to true freedom and self-determination. Simply put, we should do everything that is

3

within our power to found our own new nation. There are grave consequences if we do not.

2. The "American Dream" was never intended for most Black Americans.

- There is only one consistent and constant story for Black America—only a few achieve the "American Dream." The majority remain at the bottom in poverty. And, yes, poverty in America is a far stretch from poverty in an African, Asian, or South American nation. However, those in poverty elsewhere in the world may be better off in terms of self-worth. At least they know that they and their people own the land/nation on/in which they live. Black Americans continue to suffer the scourge of slavery and unwantedness.

This story is all too familiar. America's elites have used historical outcomes, humanistic insights, and the power of the media to determine that the "American Dream" is desirable, desired, and sought after when dangled before the unsuspecting and unknowing. To reinforce this three-layer psychological and physical trap, the elites ensure that those whom they select filter up to higher echelons of society. Colleagues, friends, and standers by, who see this transition into the world of the elite, come to believe that they, too, can realize this dream. More often than not, their preoccupation with reaching a higher economic level consumes them and their lives. When they look up from their preoccupation after 40 or 50 years of unsuccessful toil, they may still be unable to untangle the reality—only those who are hand-picked make the leap. Those who struggle for the brass ring find that it still eludes them at death. If they come to their senses before death, they realize that they should have played the game differently (economic salvation is not earned, rather it is given by the lord to his anointed), or should have played a different game altogether. Life may have been more appealing, in the end, had they settled for mediocrity and a life of fulfilled small achievements.

Of course, a life of mediocrity, even poverty, in America is a far cry from poverty elsewhere in the world. Imagine eking out a living for yourself and your family on the equivalent of two, three, or four dollars a day. There are few-to-no cases of this nature in the good old US of A. If you keep your nose clean and do the right thing, there are programs that will ensure that you have food, clothing, and shelter. Your accoutrements of life are likely to include a color television (flat screen), air conditioning, a dishwasher, and a personal computer. If you are lucky, you may even gain access to an automobile, which also has air conditioning, power windows, power brakes, and an automatic transmission. Given these life comforts, why should anyone bust their balls? The lord giveth, and the lord taketh away. The lord extends your monthly stipend, and the lord taketh it away in return for your consumption of the goods that he has produced. The problem is that you are consuming, but you are dead. You have no life of your own, the type of life intended for man, who must struggle for bread—producing, creating, imagining, fulfilling, and dealing. All of these attributes are reserved for the lord. You are less than a single centipede in a desert of loneliness.

For the poor in other God-believing countries, there is redemption even in their poverty. They struggle, produce through farming or other means, imagine a higher and brighter future for their posterity on the land that they own or control, fulfill their dreams each year of a harvest, and deal that harvest away to the lords of their country. Yet their lives are better than yours in America. At least they know that their land and their nation belong to people who look like them. Their people may not be in full control of their nation, but there is always the prospect that someones will awaken and operationalize a strategy to kick the devils out, retake the country, and return complete control of the country to the indigenous people. Under this scenario, things may not be perfect, but at least there is the prospect of control of one's life in order to produce, create, imagine, fulfill, and deal.

None of this is possible for most Blacks in America. There is no hope of retaking control, because we have never had control of America as we know it. We have controlled small settlements up and down and across this great land. That may be our only hope and strategy. That is, Black Americans may one day scratch out land for ourselves that we can control and manage for ourselves and by ourselves. It may be a small settlement within the confines of these United States. But if we can grasp such land, it would be the start of something big. It would be a place where we can fashion and materialize our own American dream—something that does not return us to the American nightmare that we live today.

3. The BEST solution to Black America's problem is separation.

- The separation of Whites from Black Americans was taught by Abraham Lincoln, Martin Robison Delany, Marcus Garvey, The Honorable Elijah Muhammad, Malcolm X (El-Hajj Malik El-Shabazz), and Minister Louis Farrakhan. All of the Black proponents of separation (nation formation) were fought by the American system. On the other hand, White Americans have a vision of the world—they want to produce, and they need consumers. They use Black Americans and poor people around the world to consume the goods that they produce, just to actualize the world economic system. Everybody can eat, but Whites will eat and have the most.

As an introduction to this commentary, let us start from a religious perspective. If you are among those who believe, as some believe, that the history of the Black man in America is presaged by the story of the Hebrews in Egypt, then you link closely the story of the Jews to the story of Black Americans. As the story goes, Moses initiates the separation of the Jews from the Egyptians under the authority of Yahweh. But let us not forget that an earlier and important portion of Moses' story is that, to avoid the wrath of the Pharoah, he escaped Egypt because he killed an Egyptian soldier who was physically abusing a Jew. While in exile from Egypt, Moses meets Yahweh, and the rest is history. What we must ask is whether, in the 21st century, some Black American will reenact the story of Moses by killing a White American policeman who is abusing a Black American, then go into exile and find Black America's God?

If you believe the foregoing Bible and Quranic story, then you will also identify with the Biblical directive to "...come out from among them, and be ye separate saith the Lord" (2nd Corinthians, 6:17). The context for this edict is for the righteous to separate from the wicked. In an American History frame of reference, are not Black Americans the righteous who have endured persecution? Are not White Americans the wicked—those who imposed evil outcomes on Black Americans? Consequently, should not Black Americans separate?

Let us now consider the issue from another American historical perspective. From the very outset, certain White and Black leaders tried to convince Black Americans of the one workable solution that is truly favorable for Black Americans—separation. First consider the role of the American Colonization Society (ACS), which was initiated in 1820. It was designed to move free Blacks in America back to Africa during the *ante bellum* period—a type of separation. By the time we get to Abraham Lincoln in the middle of the 19th century, we find that he also has separation as a central tenet of his plan for Black slaves. He tries to convince Black leadership of his plan to move the slaves to what is now Central America. The Black leadership— including Frederick Douglass—disagreed, thinking that the United States was a place where Black Americans could grow and prosper. Of course, Frederick Douglass, himself, was living a fine life as a spokesperson for Black America and benefitting from the largess of White domestic and international donors who supported the slaves' cause. Nevertheless, Abraham Lincoln, despite opposition from Black leadership, took it upon himself to test his own ideas by inaugurating what turned out to be a tragic Chiriquí Plan.

There were several Black American leaders in the 19th and 20th centuries who advocated that Black Americans should separate. Martin Robison Delany, aka the Father of Black Nationalism, was one of them. He argued long and hard for separation, but was never able to motivate separation on a large scale.

In the 20th century, Marcus Garvey was one of the first and most notable of Black American proponents of separation. As you know, he reinvigorated the back-to-Africa movement. He raised a considerable amount of funds and built a large following, but he was indicted (falsely) and deported by the U.S. Government for mail fraud before he could operationalize the movement fully. Hence, other than those who went to Africa under the ACS or under the direct control of the US Government, very few Black Americans found their way back to Africa before the 1960s.

Probably the most formidable proponent of Black American separation was the Most Honorable Elijah Muhammad—a founder and long-time leader of the Nation of Islam. Taught by Master W.D. Fard Muhammad, Elijah Muhammad taught his sizeable following various separation concepts.[2] In one case, he taught that Black Americans should occupy certain southern states. In a different case, he taught that Black Americans should ultimately emigrate to, and occupy, the area around Mecca in Saudi Arabia—the home of Muslims. Despite these seemingly conflicting messages, there is one thing about which there can be no confusion, Elijah

---

[2] To our knowledge, there is no comprehensive and definitive record on the origin and history of Master W.D. Fard Muhammad. It is beyond the scope of this commentary to provide further light on him or his role in influencing the life of Elijah Muhammad and the formation, growth, and development of the Nation of Islam.

Muhammad was a staunch advocate of Black-White separation.

While National Spokesman for the Nation of Islam during the early 1960s, the well-known Malcolm X (aka El-Hajj Malik El-Shabazz) proselytized the teachings of Elijah Muhammad concerning separation. Even when Malcolm X was excommunicated from the Nation of Islam and initiated the Organization of Afro-American Unity, he continued to preach the potential benefits of Black Americans separating from White Americans and going back to Africa.

While some may argue that Elijah Muhammad's son and successor, Wallace Deen Mohammed, took the Nation of Islam movement off course by teaching that Black Americans should adopt Orthodox Islam, he, in essence, supported a type of return to the center of Islam, which is recognized as Mecca, Saudi Arabia. In many respects, this is consistent with his father's teaching.

Another successor to Elijah Muhammad and the current leader of the Nation of Islam, Minister Louis Farrakhan, has been somewhat less pointed about separation until late. Now he is advocating that Black Americans adopt a "separation in-place" strategy; i.e., that Black Americans should come to own and control the communities in which we live—to the exclusion of non-Black Americans.[3]

---

[3] While Farrakhan's ideas are sound logically, his use of the term "community" is, in our opinion, self-defeating. Community infers small in size and insignificant. Given a nearly 50 million population, Black Americans can in no way be considered small or insignificant. Therefore, we prefer to use the term "area of influence" which has a less inimical connotation.

A third successor of Elijah Muhammad, Silis Muhammad serves as leader of the Lost Found Nation of Islam. He, too, has taught separation from America, and his organization has formed a separate Black American national government. Recently, Silis Muhammad and some of his followers emigrated to the Caribbean.

As a sign concerning the most favorable position on separation from a White American perspective, it is important to note that most White leaders who supported separation were opposed by Black Americans. In addition, at least beginning in the 20th century, all Black leaders who advocated separation were opposed vehemently by White Americans. By the time we reach the 20th century, White America realized the many economic benefits that are associated with Black Americans' presence in the country. Initially, the benefits were mainly associated with cheap labor. Later, Whites came to realize that they could make the nation's economy turn using Black Americans as a large consumer base. Hence, from the onset of the 20th century forward, White Americans—particularly elites—have desired to keep Black Americans around because they are enriching.

Actually, this reality has been transformed into an international phenomenon. Europeans the world over recognize themselves as controllers of the world economy. They serve as the master designers of economic outcomes. They control much of the financing and serve as key investors that push production to the cheapest labor markets. In certain cases, Black, Brown, Red, and Yellow people of the world can participate in the production, but they are not permitted to own the associated physical or financial capital (wealth)—other than possibly the land where the production occurs. Rather, the Black, Brown, Red, and Yellow people of the world are programmed to develop a materialism mentality, which causes them to crave consumption of the material goods that are designed and produced by the Western world. The non-Western world is allowed to earn and grow income mainly for consumption purposes; but they are not allowed to accumulate large volumes of wealth. The sad reality is that, in their haste to consume and enjoy all things Western, the world's people of color may actually be experiencing a diminution in their quality of life.[4]

Black Americans are in this very boat in the US. Hence, if we ever want to achieve a status of wealth, financial power, and control of our own destiny, America is not the place for us. Our best chance is to separate. The only economic issue about which we must decide when the question of separation is raised is: Do we want to forever be producing and consuming slaves in America, or, while experiencing somewhat lower levels of well-being, do we want to make an effort to control our own destiny by consuming the goods that we produce for ourselves—thereby generating physical and financial wealth of our own?

---

[4] The diminution in the quality of life is observable in the rapid increase in congestion in urban areas in the developing world (think significantly elongated commutes); in the increased competition for goods and services, which creates inflation and the related large shoe leather costs; in the fall in health quality that results from replacing the consumption of mainly natural foods with consumption of sugary and processed foods that are known to be detrimental to good health; and in the deterioration in environmental quality, which contributes to a rise in mortality rates.

4. Why is separation the BEST solution?

- We are due reparations—land is the only factor of value that the US Government has to offer Black Americans. The US is over 18 trillion dollars in debt, but has land. Black Americans should seek the transfer of land in pursuit of reparatory justice.

The United Nation's Human Rights Council released a report on August 18, 2016 stating that Black Americans are due reparatory justice from the United States of America.[5] The report highlights the fact that the US has been a rogue state when it comes to acceding to international treaties and accords that require guaranteed delivery of human rights to a country's citizens.

Some argue that it is this conscious failure on the part of the US that is responsible, at least in part, for events and circumstances that are unfolding in the country and around the world, which serve as adverse outcomes for America. Whether it be droughts, floods, hurricanes, snowstorms, hailstorms, or fires, America is paying for her inhumanity to Black Americans—historically and today. The pain and suffering will continue until the country acquiesces and agrees that reparatory justice for Black Americans is the order of the day.

Unfortunately for America, when this happens the nation will be in such a financial crises and debt burdened that it will not be able to offer financial assets to justly deserving

---

[5] United Nations. (2016) *Report of the Working Group of Experts on People of African Descent on its Mission to the United States of America*. Human Rights Council. Thirty-third Session, Agenda Item 9. August.

Black Americans. In fact, any public announcement of an agreement to commit to reparatory justice for Black Americans in the form of a wealth transfer, unless explicitly linked to land, will cause financial markets to tumble and roll dramatically. America's debt level is already teetering on a precipice that can motivate debt rating downgrades. The act of adding a substantial amount of new debt in the form of trillions of dollars, would create conditions for a financial crash in the US. Fortunately for Black Americans, the US will be able to offer nonfinancial assets—mainly in the form of land to settle the claim. In fact, if the US attempts to offer financial assets (particularly cash), the offer should be rejected out of hand. What we need that is of value is wealth in the form of land.

The transfer of land from the US Government to Black Americans should be conducted under very strict protocols such that the land cannot be sold to non-Black Americans into perpetuity. Once designated Black American soil, it should remain such down through history.

Given land, Black Americans can begin our development as a new nation with bright aspirations and sound strategies. We can create a place where Black Americans can live in peace and harmony, while striving with the highest level of excellence to produce a model nation that enables the world to evolve to a new level of human existence.

- The nation continues to prove that Black and White Americans cannot get along; viz., the police brutality, economic discrimination, and the race war that we are on the verge of experiencing because of a limited number of jobs. Whites will go to war with Black Americans over jobs.

Given a long-standing existence of a racist society, how long does it take for that society to become nonracist? America has had nearly 400 years to achieve this outcome—i.e., since the advent of Africans into North America (according to American History) in 1619. One might argue that all of America, the North and the South, began agonizing over the question of race with the conclusion of the Civil War in 1865. Hence, America has been on a path toward a nonracist society for 151 years. Agreed, there have been some social adjustments. A certain percentage (the proverbial 10 percent) of Black Americans have been able to filter up into the higher echelons of American society. Even more have reached the middle class in income terms. However, when it boils right down to it, and when confronted with the question of who should be granted the better outcome, how many Whites are willing to defer to Blacks? In other words, on a level playing field, with both parties in dire need of an opportunity to work and survive in America, how many Whites are truly willing to agree that their chance at employment should not exceed the chance of a Black American? What is clear is that over 25 percent of Black Americans live in poverty in America today, while only 10 percent of Whites experience this pernicious evil. Notably, we have not even touched on the huge wealth gap and the question of whether any Whites would ever be willing to give up some of their wealth so that wealth inequality could be reduced. As opposed to asking "how long," maybe we should ask, "Can America ever dispense with its racist ways?" Will there always be competition between Blacks and Whites with Blacks experiencing the adverse outcome?

We have answered this question with the statement that "All it Takes is One."[6] In other words, whenever, and as long as, two groups live together (an "in-group" and an "out-group") where the history of the two groups includes periods of pain and abuse being imposed by the in-group on the out-group, all it takes is for one person from the out-group to remember the past and issue a cry for justice (and incite others to join in that cry), and there is a significant probability that violence between the two groups will ensue. On the other hand, if the out-group receives favor and rises above the ingroup, then all it takes is for one in-group member to remember the group's former position of superiority and issues a cry for a return to the old status quo, then there, too, is a significant probability that violence between the two groups will ensue.

Stated differently, we believe that only if the two groups can be brought to a state of pure equality (in all respects), and the history completely and totally erased, can the two groups ever expect to live in peace and harmony for an extended period of time. However, because the evils of history will always be archived in libraries and in other written and oral forms, it is impossible to prevent the reality of the past from surfacing and sparking violence for justice or for a return to the old status quo.

---

[6] B.B. Robinson. (2012) "All it Takes is One." A BlackEconomics.org Essay. Retrieved on October 4, 2016; http://www.blackeconomics.org/BELit/AITIO.pdf.

Given these realities, we believe that the logical answer is that a society that is once stamped as racist, will always be racist—one side against the other. This racism may be subtle, submerged below the surface, but always there.

In America today, we are experiencing the *nth* resurrection of the cry for justice and for a return to the status quo. Black Lives Matter and other movements are calling for justice, while America's policemen and Trumpites are calling for a maintenance of the status quo—Black men dead in the streets like dogs, just as we were hung from trees all across America, but especially the South, during the Jim Crow Era. Recently, the story of Emmit Till surfaced again, and the pain was excruciating like salt in an open wound. At the same time, there is the ongoing fear by some Whites that Black Americans will rise up and commit the type of violence fostered upon Whites by the likes of Nathaniel Turner.

Actually, history is the real problem because it can never be overcome. Even though Whites know that they have done an excellent job of sublimating hate against them by their former slaves through Jesus Teachings, Islam in America (particularly the teachings of the Honorable Elijah Muhammad) has unwound the Jesus Teachings, and is realigning Black Americans away from our pacifist leanings and more toward the Old Testament and Quranic Teachings of *Lex Talionis*; an eye for an eye, a tooth for a tooth, a life for a life. As one proponent of Islam put it, the Islamic seed is a powerful seed. Therefore, Whites fear that they can no longer trust their former slaves to love them despite the historical and current spiteful abuse of Blacks by Whites.

It really is a simple calculus. Blacks are becoming more educated and aware of the world and the role of the European in it. We see ourselves at the bottom of humanity's heap. We have explored the reasons for that position, and are willing to strike out against Whites because of the centuries of unimaginable wrongs perpetrated against and upon us. At the same time, Whites fear that if Blacks ever reach a position of superiority—in any way—then we will teach the lesson of "what goes around comes around." That is Whites fear that Blacks will perpetrate the same evils against Whites that Whites perpetrated against Blacks. Honestly, they are warranted in their fears.

In simplest terms, when two sides live with the perpetual potential of war, they can never live together in peace. Separation is the answer!

To prevent Black Americans from rising and imposing our will on Whites, Whites have adopted a rock solid position on discrimination, racism, and White supremacy. One of the easiest avenues for Black Americans to rise is to capture jobs, earn income, and accumulate wealth. Whites want to prevent this at all cost. Whites camouflage this position by permitting a filtering of a small percentage of Blacks up the economic ladder, while ensuring that the majority of Blacks are out of work, in jail, or are working jobs that permit mere economic survival in the American system. Consequently, any attempt by the US Government to actually enforce antidiscrimination laws has been, and will be, met by strong opposition from White America and the onset of a race war blood bath that Malcolm X predicted over 50 years ago.

- Economically, separation is the most feasible and reasonable solution for Black Americans. In our own nation, we will need to produce goods and services that will create jobs for us; thereby, eliminating our own unemployment. Our absence from the US could create jobs for Whites in America who may be underemployed, but it would open up a huge chasm in America's consumption base. We are proving continuously that we know how to operate businesses—we just cannot grow those businesses large enough to hire employees and reduce unemployment because of being swallowed up by larger White firms and/or we are permitted insufficient access to capital. These problems are easily resolved in a new nation for Black America.

When we call for separation, we are invoking a very favorable outcome on Black Americans and a severely unfavorable outcome on White Americans.

Economics is at the root of almost all Black American problems. Add more income and wealth to any regression equation that attempts to explain Black America's adverse outcomes, and the outcomes change favorably. No matter how you slice it, separation may mean a temporary reduction in physical well-being for Black Americans, but in the long run, separation means the addition of income and wealth to the equation, which portends very favorable outcomes for Black Americans.

How will the income and wealth be generated? First, a significant amount of wealth will be transferred when reparatory justice is imposed. Second, a considerable amount of new physical wealth can be created when Black

Americans develop the infrastructure required to meet our needs in a separate territory. The process of creating the infrastructure and performing the services that are required by Black Americans in the new territory will create income, which, too, can be transformed into wealth. This is not to say that there will be no leakages from the circular flow of income and wealth; there will be a need to import certain goods and services—at least initially. However, we should also be able to produce certain goods and services to attract foreign inflows of income, which can be used to produce more wealth. The central point to keep in mind is that, if we design our economy correctly, we can use most of the available labor in our new nation productively—something that has not occurred in the US since slavery. A very favorable outcome for Black Americans indeed.

In fact, if one tracks the growth of Black-owned businesses in the US through the Census Bureau's Survey of Business Owners and Self-Employed Persons, one finds that Black Americans have a very strong and growing entrepreneurial spirit. We know how to create very small businesses that are owner-operated. Success at creating many small owner-operated businesses portends the survival of some of these businesses, which should grow to become large businesses with employees. Black businesses in the US fail to grow primarily for two reasons: (1) They are swallowed up by large and established White firms; and (2) they are denied access to capital with which to expand. With at least one of these hurdles surmounted within a separate Black nation, we should expect Black Americans businesses to thrive, grow, and help keep our unemployment rate to a minimum.

Observing the other side of the coin, we should ask: "Which is the most feared outcome for Western or developed economies?" The answer is: "A declining population!" As you know, population growth is an important guarantor of economic growth. When population ceases to grow, there is a high probability that, unless productivity accelerates rapidly, economic growth will decelerate and then decline. Japan knows what this looks like today. South Korea will face this problem soon. Without immigration from Africa, the Caribbean, Asia, and the Middle-East, Europe would be facing this outcome too. Consequently, when we talk about Black Americans separating from the United States, we are talking about a massive fall in the US population and, thereby, a large reduction in the level and growth of the US economy. It will be impossible for the US to bring immigrants in fast enough to fill the gap created by a Black American exodus.

But some clouds have a silver lining. White Americans, who were under-employed or unemployed before separation, may find that they can fill jobs left vacant by Black Americans due to separation. Obviously, these Whites will favor separation. However, elite Whites, who are the financers and owners of production, will find separation abhorrent because it will wash away the large Black consumption base that has guaranteed above-normal profits during each economic cycle.

Given the temporary reduction in well-being and the imbalance in economic outcomes, we should expect that certain Black and White Americans will push back very hard on the idea of separation being an entry in Black America's choice set. However, we should be hasty in choosing to produce the best outcome in our own long-term interests. If we do not, as we will see later in this set of commentaries, Black Americans will find that we will have missed the final opportunity for self-determination and nationhood in this historical dispensation.

- As a nation with the knowledge that we have concerning the tricknology of White America, we serve as a check against White Supremacy for the world—something that must evolve if the world is to endure for the long run.

Black Americans should be self-indicting. Why? Because since the 17th century at least, we have enabled America's rise. What has that meant for the world? It has meant US support for White Supremacy the world over, which, in turn, means suppression of progress among the majority of the world's Black, Brown, Red, and Yellow populations. It is true that a Yellow people, the Japanese, experienced a rise during the 20th century leading up to World War II. However, Black Americans enabled the US to squelch that rise, along with the rise of the Germans in complete and total defeat. It was on the back of Black Americans that America then turned to the Germans (practically all of Western Europe) and the Japanese to help rebuild those societies following the war.

It is also true that another Yellow people, the South Koreans, have also risen during the latter half of the 20th century. However, that rise was enabled, again, on the backs of Black Americans because the US invested tremendously in South Korea following the Korean War.

Let us not forget the Chinese. They too benefitted at the expense of Black Americans when the United States, led by the "vision" of Richard Nixon, initiated support for China's rise through "State Capitalism" during the 1970s, 1980s, and 1990s.

Even the brown (South Asian) Indians have benefitted at the expense of Black Americans. How? Starting in the 1950s, the Indians began to model their Indian Institutes of Technology (IIT) after the Massachusetts Institute of Technology (MIT) with the help of the United States. After beginning to develop in scientific fields, and obtaining opportunities from the White Russians, India developed important manufacturing techniques, which has enabled its slow rise.

Why do we say that all of these nations were able to benefit at Black Americans' expense? Because, throughout the entire period, Black Americans continued to serve as a cheap source of labor and as a large consumption base that enabled White American businesses to earn above-normal profits that could be invested in these other countries. In addition, the US Government was able to minimize its expenditures on Black Americans relative to what should have been spent to enable our rise, and use those resources to help American businesses abroad in the form of military support or in the form of aid—both can be read to mean that American businesses benefitted and helped foreign countries benefit at the same time.

It is all a grand scheme that enables US infiltration of other countries with the intent of influencing the culture—selling a culture and making the world want everything US. This, in turn, permits American firms to sell to the rest of the world their goods and services and continue to grow richer and gain greater material and psychological control over these other parts of the world.

Malcolm X argued that there were "Field Negroes" and "House Negroes." We expand this tradition to say that all

Black Americans are House Negroes vis-à-vis the rest of the world. We have taken up a seat in this White House called America, eaten the crumbs from the rich man's table like dogs, and supported White America in her effort to gain complete control of the parts of the world that she has valued. Once under America's grip, it is almost impossible to recover—unless minds are remade, ears and eyes are reopened, and tastes are changed.

It is only among Black Americans that one can find the medicine men and women who have the knowledge and power required to remake the world by enabling the world to hear, see, and taste that which is ordained for man if we all expects to survive as human beings (as we know ourselves today) on the planet.

The world has seen, and Black Americans have been in a position to comprehend, that the European mentality is all about materialism—something to do with the short growing seasons experienced during the early stages of civilization in Europe. The European mentality is to design a new product and get it to market before a competitor does—irrespective of the potential harm that it may create for humans or for the environment. Also, Schumpeter's "creative destruction" is part and parcel of the European mentality. In other words, do not worry about killing and destroying because such death and destruction create opportunities for renewal and economic growth. Planned obsolescence is another component of the European mentality—no matter how wasteful. One of the latest elements of the European mentality is to design defective products and place them on the market and then cause consumers to not only purchase the defective products, but to also purchase secondary products that enable the defective product to function—at least temporarily; viz., computers and the related software, which only function if they are protected by anti-virus software. And we have not even begun to mention the products that are designed to kill consumers outright. The power of advertisement and the quest for consumption is so great that consumers are forced to purchase these products addictively; e.g., tobacco products that cause cancer and sugary products that often lead to obesity and diabetes—all of which places one on a path to death.

The European mind is quite a deviant mind. It evolved a new meaning for the word "commerce." Whereas commerce, 300 or 400 years ago, used to mean to produce and sell/exchange a reliable good or service, the word now means to produce and sell anything that you can trick some greater fool into purchasing. Nothing is real. Nothing is honest. Nothing is fair. Nothing is righteous. This is tricknology at its worst.

Notably, this interpretation of the European/White American economic and commercial systems that are operating today was enabled by the very unique vantage point held by Black Americans. Fortunately, for the world, there are hints of this type of understanding and interpretation emerging on a more global scale. The world is beginning to recognize that many things European/White American or Western represent a certain road to death and destruction. In order to remove the world from this destructive path, it is critical for the world to realize and adopt a new path. Given our unique perspective, Black Americans should be able to help shift the world to this new path.

How can Black Americans help the world save itself? The first step is to exodus the United States of America and found our own new nation. It is in the safety, security, and nurturing environment of the new nation that this emerging Black mind can form completely and then be prepared to help raise (resurrect) the world from the death and destruction that confronts us today politically, economically, and environmentally.

5. Blacks cannot govern ourselves.

    •   This lie has proven itself false many times already. We cannot govern ourselves when Whites infiltrate our spheres of influence; otherwise, we govern ourselves well. In any event, it is more joyous to live in a slightly malfunctioning nation of our own than to continue living in an evil and cruel United States of America.

Today, successful "governance" conjures up the idea of a society that is well-endowed materially. We see here again the old European emphasis on wealth and materialism. Please do not get us wrong. There is nothing inherently incorrect or wrong about having plenty. However, there is a problem when there is too much or too little.

Probably a more efficacious interpretation of successful governance would focus on how well a society operates with respect to meeting its basic requirements, but also on how well the society functions. One could simply ask: Is there calm, peace, and prosperity in the society? A society that may be most emblematic of the latter conditions would be a society without the need for a jail. Such a society would be expected to have calm and no anger that causes violent behavior; and prosperity that is well distributed so that the poor do not feel obliged to take what they need violently. Have there ever been such societies? Yes, of course? Which societies were they?

In our cursory study of this topic, we have identified at least two such societies. First, on the East Coast of the African Continent where the language Swahili was spoken as part of a largely Muslim culture until the coming of the European, the language did not even include a word for jail.[7] Second, the Mauri people, particularly the Hawaiians, had such peaceful societies that they, too, did not have jails.[8] Did not citizens of those societies commit crimes? Most likely. However, the society was structured in such a way that it was not necessary to impose inhuman treatment on humans. Jails inflict inhuman treatment. By the way, both of these were societies of Black people. Apparently, these Black cultures knew how to govern themselves well.

Black Americans have also shown a strong ability and proclivity to govern well. For example, following the Civil War many Black Americans migrated west and formed scores of small all-Black towns, which operated well.[9] They mainly encountered difficulty when they were infiltrated by Whites, who exhibited envy and hate against the Blacks because of the prosperity that they had been able to generate from their material environment.[10]

It is instructive to observe this pattern of successful development before infiltration by Whites who are bent on destroying Black success. It is common knowledge that

---

[7] See page xviii of Thomas J. Hinnebusch Sarah M. Mirza, and Adelheid U. Stein (1998), Kiswahili/Swahili, 2nd Edition. University Press of America, Inc. Lanham, MD.

[8] This condition was cited as part of an oral history of Hawaii by a native Hawaiian circa 2012.

[9] Quintard Taylor. (1998) *In Search of the Racial Frontier: African Americans in the American West 1528-1990*, W.W. Norton & Company, New York, NY.

[10] An important and well-known example of White rage against a successful Black population in America's West is the story of the 1921 riot on Black Wall Street in Tulsa, Oklahoma. See Danney Goble's (2000), *Final Report of the Commission to Study the Tulsa Race Riot of 1921*, Commission to Study the Tulsa Race Riot of 1921, Tulsa, OK.

Marcus Garvey's Universal Negro Improvement Association and Elijah Muhammad's Nation of Islam were very successful and well governed organizations prior to the FBI's infiltration of the groups. Similarly, the Black Panther Party was also an effective organization until the FBI began to tamper with the organization's operations. In fact, a study of the history of Black movements in America will show that such groups generally make solid progress in organizing and operating until the FBI infiltrates the organizations with the aim of destroying them.

Crossing the Atlantic, one finds Black sub-Saharan nations struggling to govern themselves effectively. A thorough and sound analysis of the governance in these nations is likely to reveal, as in the US case, that these nations would be more successful at governance if they were left to their own devices. It turns out that, since achieving "independence" in the 1950s and 1960s, these nations have been bombarded with influence from outside—if not foreign governments, then foreign business. The latter indicate that they intend to help these nations' economies grow. However, these firms and their governments are complicit in engendering corrupt practices, which causes divisiveness. The divisiveness leaves the Africans fighting over crumbs, while foreigners walk away with resources.

Therefore, we believe that it is safe to say that, when left unattended, Black people manage to govern themselves effectively. This is not to say that perfect societies have evolved or would evolve. However, if one could roll back the clock and restore the naturally God-fearing and religious mentality of Blacks before the European materialistic mind gained currency, it seems reasonable that Blacks would produce wholesome societies that function well.

And even if Black nations experience less than perfect governance, there is something joyous to be said for living with and among people who look, think, talk, and act like our own Black selves—at least when the White Supremacist mentality has not pervaded the society. However, if we ever want to get to this point, then we are going to have to figure how to exclude the White mind from the Black environment. A Black nation with knowing leadership is the best path for achieving this outcome.

6.　If we do not separate?

- There will be a river of blood; or Black blood,
as we know it, will cease to flow.

Life itself and the art of living are evolutionary processes. When Europeans went to Africa to steal souls to serve as very low-cost labor to enrich themselves, that alone was their immediate focus. But soon, Whites in America began to realize that Black slaves would become a very problematic species of property. And so began the continuous evolutionary process of creating strategies for controlling, destroying, and amalgamating Black Americans.[11] We emphasize continuous because, even at this time in the 21st century, wealthy White Americans continues to evolve strategies designed to produce these ends. For the moment, they control Black (and poor White) minds with the media and miseducation; they destroy Blacks (and poor Whites) with wars, drugs, gang murders, jails, and police murder; and they amalgamate Black Americans by convincing us to love what is White so much and to hate Black so much that fully

---

[11] Central to this strategy was the imposition of "White Supremacy," which originates as a mental/psychological phenomenon. "White Supremacy" superimposes Whiteness over Blackness in the minds of Black Americans. So much so that, even after experiencing higher incomes and greater wealth than many Whites, Blacks are likely to retain a mindset of inferiority (sublimation) to Whites. Reversing this mindset/consciousness can only be accomplished by separation from imposers of "White Supremacy," and an awakening of self-actualization in a safe and secure environment. It is only in the context of a self-supporting and self-reliant environment that Black Americans can come to recognize ourselves as equals to citizens of other nations of the world—be they Red, Yellow, Brown, Black, or White. After overthrowing "White Supremacy" bondage, Black Americans can take our rightful place in the world, and perform our special and very important role in the world.

25 percent of Black males marry outside of our race.[12] If you are a student of the media, then you will also be awake to the reality that there is an increasing media message for Black females to marry White males.

It is important to recognize that the control and destroying strategies are engendering a considerable amount of animus between Blacks and Whites. Given these strategies and the morass in the US economy with what will become declining jobs, we are likely to experience an escalation of tensions to the point of running and violent battles in the country between Blacks and Whites. Because Whites are so much more prepared for combat than Blacks, Black blood promises to flow liberally in the streets of America. This is likely to be true the greater is the probability that the nation's political leadership reflects a Trump-like mentality.

Now to the amalgamation strategy, which is the genetic blending of Blackness and Whiteness. Typically, the pairing of Black and White partners produces offspring whose phenotype is a mixture; part Black and part White. In the American society, persons with such a (light skin) phenotype enjoy more favorable socio-economic outcomes than Black Americans whose skin color is dark.[13] The psychological explanation for this outcome is that light-skinned Black Americans have a close resemblance to White Americans, and it is common knowledge that humans naturally prefer to

---

[12] Wendy Wang, (2015). "Interracial Marriages: Who's Marrying Out?" Pew Research Center. June. Retrieved from the Internet on October 9, 2016; http://www.pewresearch.org/fact-tank/2015/06/12/interracialmarriage-who-is-marrying-out/.

[13] Goldsmith, Arthur H., Hamilton, Darrick, and Darity, William A. Jr. (2007) "From Dark to Light: Skin Color and Wages among African-Americans." *Journal of Human Resources*. Vol. 42; No. 4; pp. 701-38.

socialize with those who think, behave, and look similar to themselves.

Taking this analysis one step further, if light-skinned persons partner with Whites, then the resulting offspring have a significant probability of a White-like phenotype. Such a phenotype enables smooth integration into White society. Given a very slow population growth rate for Whites compared with much of the rest of the world, it is this amalgamation process that permits Europeans and White Americans to increase the population of people who at least have the appearance of Whiteness.[14] Also, this amalgamation helps to ensure against a significant reduction in the European and White American share of the world's population.

As a captive population, which is conditioned to adore, even seek, whiteness, Black Americans are central to this strategy. Therefore, if we do not separate from White America, then Black blood as we know it today will cease to flow given sufficient time and amalgamation.

Simply put, in America, if Black Americans seek to oppose control and destroy strategies, then we face the hatred of White America and the prospect of violence and death. And if we succumb to the amalgamation strategies, then we will find ourselves disappearing from the world. Our only reasonable choice is to separate now before it is too late. We have endured too much, and survived too long, to simply

---

[14] Akkoc, Raziye. (2015) "How Europe is Slowly Dying Despite an Increasing World Population." *The Telegraph*. February 16th. Retrieved from the Internet on October 12, 2016;
http://www.telegraph.co.uk/news/worldnews/11414064/How-Europe-is-slowly-dying-despite-an-increasing-world-population.html.

cease to exist. We are a durable people who have overcome much. However, Western World science is becoming increasingly powerful, and if we do not escape its reach, then we will find that the period of our future survival may be limited. Our best hope and strategy is to separate and form a new nation that can seek to guarantee our survival into perpetuity.

7. Do not Black Americans deserve our own nation right here in America?

- Before the advent of the European, we enjoyed the rights and privileges of full-fledged citizenship. Other peoples have been able to overcome slavery and form their own nation. We have played, and will continue to play, a special role in the history of the world. The script for the next act in world history calls for nation formation for Black Americans.

Before we were dragged from the continent of Africa, placed in the holes of ships, and ferried across the Atlantic Ocean to America, we were citizens of villages, tribes, kingdoms, or nations. Why do we not deserve to enjoy the full and natural rights of citizenship again? Clearly, America is not very interested in making us true and fully integrated citizens in this White man's land. Therefore, should we not be permitted to form a land/nation of our own?

We cannot return to Africa, neither do we want to. In several respects, Africans are worse off than Black Americans. Africans have less disposable material wealth on average, they are less educated on average, and they have not lived the extraordinarily close experience of sitting at the feet of Whites to learn the ways of the modern world that Black Americans have lived. On the other hand, Africans are better off than Black Americans because, as we have already discussed, at least they have a certain prospect of turning the table on outsiders and retaking their land for themselves. Consequently, the most likely location of settlement for a new Black American nation is in North America.

If the small group known to the world today as Jews deserve a homeland, then do not Black Americans deserve the same? As discussed earlier, Black Americans often associate ourselves with the Biblical Hebrew tradition; i.e., serving as slaves under a hard task master for 430 years, then an Exodus to form a nation that is blessed by God. By adopting this historical role as our own, we are saying that we, too, deserve land to build our own nation because we, too, are blessed by God.

In certain parts of Eastern Europe, there are ethnic groups that have carved out national space for themselves after serving mainly as serfs (serfdom is only different from slavery by a mere technicality) in what was the Russian Empire during the 17th through 19th centuries. Today, they enjoy the security of nation state status: Consider Lithuania, Belarus, Ukraine, etc. If they deserve their own homeland, do not Black Americans deserve the same?

Consider South Sudan and the very recent (2011) formation of a new African nation. The formation of this new nation reflects the South Sudanese's efforts to benefit economically from the natural resources resident in their territory. However, it also reflects a fight for liberation and freedom from religious oppression and, in certain cases, physical slavery. If the 10 million South Sudanese were justified in forming their own nation, are not Black Americans equally justified?[15]

---

[15] Unfortunately, South Sudan has been a nation in turmoil since its founding. However, we attribute this condition, in large measure, to the type of external infiltration and tampering already discussed, which is designed to make the nation fail so that others can benefit from the spoils.

We are nearly 50 million people strong, with a wealth of academic knowledge, and practical experience on a variety of levels—economics and business, military science, politics, religion, medicine, sports and culture, and education. What we may be lacking is very pervasive knowledge of mathematics, science, and technology. However, given the opportunity to grasp these fields, there is no question that we can master them too—especially if we are forced to by circumstances.

We have what it takes to build a nation successfully—particularly if we can protect ourselves from infiltration and tampering during the development process. Today, most African nations are doing a reasonable job of governing themselves. They might perform even better governance if outsiders were removed from the equation. The latter are eternally present planting seeds of discord so that they can serve as the ultimate arbiters of peace and wellbeing. In our view, Black Americans can do even better than the Africans in creating a nation of our own because we have the latter as historical examples of what to, and what not to, do.

But we should not compare ourselves to African nations. In fact, we should not compare ourselves with any other nation because we are unique in so many ways. Rather, we must know that we are a very special people, who have been especially prepared to help transform the world. The first step on this transformation path is to organize ourselves into a solid nation that is designed to do righteousness in the world and to help initiate a new world order as the old world order dies.

This is our case for nation formation for Black Americans.

www.ingramcontent.com/pod-product-compliance
Lightning Source LLC
Chambersburg PA
CBHW070235290526
45789CB00004B/1636